POEMS, RHYMES, JOTTINGS
LOOSE SCREWS,

Poetry for the Normally – Don't Do
And everyone else

Eric C.A. Godward

ACKNOWLEDGEMENTS

With grateful thanks to Ruby and Jeanne
who had the inspiration and determination
to get this little book published.

DEDICATION

——— •●• ———

I DEDICATE THIS LITTLE BOOK
TO MY DEAR FRIEND MARY.

Florence Mary Martha Arnold,
I call to see her just about every day.

CONTENTS

Nothing's been ruled in
Nothing's been ruled out
We lost the pencil.

REFLECTION

You look in the mirror
What do you see
The reflection of someone like you.

They are different of course
As their left is your right
Reflecting an image untrue
Just so quick off the mark
In the light or the dark
Can they blink any quicker than you.

THE GOLDFISH

Bought a goldfish from a shop
Gift for our young daughter
Trouble is we soon found out
The goldfish hated water.

He sleeps upon a little shelf
Beside his rounded bowl
We wrap him up in cotton wool
To warm his little soul.

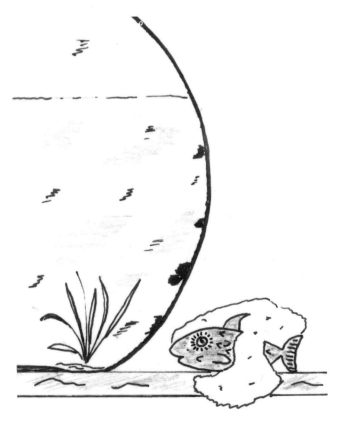

HALF

—— •●• ——

If love is half as good as this
Well give me more of that.

If love is worth just half a kiss
It's half as good as this and that.

Formula

half kiss = ki or ss

$$\text{ki or ss} \times \text{love} \ \frac{\text{this}}{\text{that}} \ = 0.5$$

THE VILLAGE SHOP

The Village Shop has much to sell
Amongst the trash there's good as well.

Unfortunately the owner's deaf
He used to be a football Ref.
The noise at football hurt his ears
He sold his whistle for some beers.
Now he's deaf and runs the shop
His sporting life just had to stop.

I wanted something to fix my tiles
He gave me ointment meant for piles.

Someone asked for a fancy knife
The owner offered up his wife.

The Village Shop has much to sell
What you get, no one can tell.

BEWARE

·●·

We must not refer to the past,
in fact, we were both never there.

Bait lines are now set and are cast,
to catch out the ones who may dare.

MY MILKMAN

My milkman hasn't got a van
He brings the milk as soon as he can.

No one ever makes a fuss
He sometimes brings it on the bus.

At times he's even had to hike
Once he came on his neighbour's bike.

My milk arrives but I know not how
All I know, it's from a cow.

ASCOT HAT

A gorgeous woman in an Ascot hat.
Naughty boy with a baseball bat.

A large policeman eating honey.
The gorgeous woman thought that was funny.

A bee then landed on her head.
Boy's baseball bat then struck it dead.

The policeman led the boy away.
The Ascot hat had had its day.

SINGING IN THE RAIN

Singing in the rain just masks the pain
Handel's Largo, like Greta Garbo
She just wants to be alone. Never phones,
Such a shame, all down the drain
This sad refrain, Singing in the Rain.

ONE SEED FROM THE PACKET

Remember where you came from.
Our life, we have to hack it.
We never choose our seed of life –
Just one seed from the packet.

Perhaps you are a mixture.
We range from frail to hunky.
Thank heavens you can read these lines.
You could have been a monkey.

BACK AWAY

One day you'll be a man my son
It's when you back away.

Those times you've played around with Dad
He let you win the day.

Now, you are a man my son
Your Dad has had his day.

You know that you are far too strong
It's time to back away.

THE VICAR AND THE MAYOR

When the Vicar comes to dinner
It is best to never swear
We entertain all sorts of guests
Once we had the Mayor.

Today is very special
Our Mayor is with the Vicar
We'll feed them well, no talk of hell
But first we hide the liquor.

We know they're up to something
Their pretence is not so stable
The Vicar and our guest the Mayor
Hold hands beneath the table.

THE GREAT GATES OF HELL

THE GREAT GATES OF HELL WERE CLOSED FOR THE DAY
VAST HINGES AND METAL CORRODED.
THE DEVIL FELT TRAPPED, THEN THUNDER CLAPPED.
HE WAS ANGRY AND MERELY EXPLODED.

A TRUCK LOAD OF DEAD JUST WAITED IN DREAD
TO ENTER THE GREAT GATES OF HELL.

GATES REMAINED CLOSED SO THE DRIVER JUST DOZED
IT WAS TIME FOR THE DEAD TO REBEL
WITH VIGOUR AND PLUCK THEY TOOK OVER THE TRUCK
THEN DROVE LIKE THE WIND BACK FROM HELL.

40 DEGREES

We watched him read his little book
His eyes fixed to the page
Then we cut his chair leg off
Peace soon turned to rage.

He still read on but the leg was gone
His nose was near his knees
The angle then was far too steep
To read at 40 Degrees.

THE KAMIKAZE PILOT

The Kamikaze Pilot
Got a ticket on a train
The conductor said Single?
Coming back again?

He left his Mum in Tokyo
A mother so concerned
"Give me a ticket
Make it out, Return"

HURT

I fell, but she was hurt
Because I fell for another.

I tried to tell, to the one I fell
Of the hurt I'd done to the other.

GOD GIVE WOMEN A CHANCE

There's a place they play cards short of heaven
At the table fake Leaders of Men
They've failed and have lost at such bitter cost
God give Women a chance to amend.

At the table they cheat, twisting minds of the weak
Who follow their doctrines and laws
God, give Women a chance so minds can advance
Then deal out these bigots and bores.

THE LIBRARY

In our Library it's plain to see
There are many books and journals
We open our doors to back street Whores
dirty Tramps and Colonels.

We've books on Sex and Oedipus Rex*
Of Chilblains and of Chaps
Some look up their diseases
A few have got the clap.

Some come in just for company
They hide away and text
Often it's much more than that
We find them having sex.

It's fun to work in the Library
It could never be a bore
And when it's time to shut up shop
We kick them out the door.

*Oedipus Rex, in Greek mythology, the
King of Thebes who killed his father
so he could marry his Mother.

COME AND SEE US

Come and see us when you can
Make sure you wipe your feet.

Let me know the month before
So there'll be food to eat.

Come and see us when you can
To stay away is better
But if you really have to come
Invite yourself by letter.

Come and see us when you can
Say when you want to stay
As long as we have time enough
To plan to run away.

BELLY BUTTON

I went to see the Doctor, it gave him a fright.
My button fell off, sometime in the night.
He searched on the net, to find what to do.
Under B that's for Belly, the answer came through.
Just stick it back on, with the aid of some glue.

CHOICE

In the womb, you are free of religion
It's your fight to survive and breathe air
Although they would say, God is with you
Young minds are not ready to care.
Your Mother, and your Father are Muslim
Or Christian, Hindu or Jew
You will need to obey, to have it their way
But one day, It is all up to you.

HEARTLESS

I left my heart in San Francisco
Next to Tony Bennett's house
When Tony went and found it
He fried it for his mouse.

BALLERINA GIRL

In the room where Mary sits
There's a picture on the wall
The picture is of Mary
Ballerina of the ball.

It was taken long ago
Between the Great World Wars
Passing years have taken toll
She now stays inside doors.

Mary was that little girl
The picture on the wall
But now a gracious lady
Who sits before she falls.

HOW?

Wondered where you came from?
Have you ever thought it out?
There's half of you from Daddy
His genes you share no doubt.

The other half is magic
For that you needed Mummy
You came alive in just nine months
To come from Mummy's tummy.

One day when you are older
Then they will tell you how
So wait until you're bigger
But that will do for now.

RUBY

Ruby is Red.

She fell in Paint

They think she's Blushing.

Oh No, she Ain't.

NODDY THE ESKIMO

Noddy is an Eskimo, he makes igloos built in packs.
They are sent around the world, but most of them
come back.

He sends them off to Congo, one he sent to Chad.
All the other Eskimos think he is raving mad.

Noddy is a family man, he has a wife and daughter.
His business is collapsing as his igloos turn to water.

BANANAS

Have you ever seen a monkey
wash his banana in a pond?
First of all he waves it,
just watch the girls respond.

They dangle their bananas
and jump from tree-to-tree.
When they get excited
it's very plain to see.

Now little boys are different,
their bananas are arousers.
But when they get excited,
at least it's in their trousers,

When you're way past ninety,
your banana goes quite limp
You think of all the times gone by
when you were just a chimp.

THE VICAR COULDN'T MAKE IT

The Vicar couldn't make it,
he did the wedding on the phone,
He was ringing from a call box
just near his flooded home.

The organ started playing,
the guests began to sing,
With the best man at the ready
to offer up the ring.

When singing was all over,
the Vicar read a psalm,
The best man still was ready,
ring firmly in his palm.

Phone lines started acting up,
the sound all cracked and funny,
The Vicar had to stop it there,
He'd just run out of money.

JUST LIKE BEFORE

He swore he'd never swear again.
Then sweared he'd never swored.
We knew he'd sweared, he does it more.
He swears and swored just like before.

WELCOME TO L.A.

It's true to say that old L.A.
Has a mix of every type
A melting pot of people
Each demanding rights.

They make the world a better place
The rights of men must stand
To walk the paths of freedom
In this their promised land.

They proudly share their style of life
And welcome you to stay
Enjoy the gift that heaven's sent
You'll hate to go away.

AUNTIE DOT

Auntie Dot rings quite a lot
She's always on the phone.
However, we just let it ring
And make out we're not home.

It's only when we have the time
At least an hour or four
Then we'll talk and talk and talk
It seems for evermore.

Auntie Dot rings quite a lot
She's sweet, a dear old thing
However, she just drives us mad
With that ring, ring, ring, ring, ring.

RESPECT

Marketing is quite an art

The trends they must reflect

However, it's impossible

To sell or buy respect.

REMI

Allergic to dust, can't stand a loud noise.
This lad who's autistic, don't play with the boys.
Though food is a problem and habits are many.
His mother will love him, her first child, her Remi.
She fights for his future, there are days that she dreads.
Some days are so awful, she cries in her bed.
A mother who's single, there's so much to do.
Now longs for vacations and pastures anew.
A boy who's autistic, what futures to come?
He's lucky, there's someone, his life is his Mum.

THE LADY OF THE NIGHT

She was a lady of the night.
It was twice in every week.
Always left at midnight
Through curtains we did peek.

Always on a Monday.
Often Thursdays too.
We wondered where she really went
But then we never knew.

One day we saw her in her Jag .
Clutching at her shopping bag.
No longer do we stop to peek.
She still does shopping twice a week..

SUPER GLUE

I went to bed with a severed head,
Just coughed and it fell off.
Trouble is my super glue
Is somewhere in the loft.

If I don't find this super glue
Don't really know what else to do.
Now, I think I've lost my comb
Today I think I'll stay at home.

IT RAINED

——— ·•· ———

It rained so hard I took a bus, then I took a train.

The police came round and locked me up..

THE GREAT DEPRESSION
———— •●• ————

During the Great Depression of the early 1930's
my whole family were out of work and very poor.
So my Grandfather sacrificed his wooden leg to put
on the fire so the rest of the family could keep warm.
Unfortunately, the chimney caught fire and the house
burnt down so were homeless.
They never ever forgave him for that

HORLICKS

The House of Lords debated
That they should stop for drinks
Some preferred to stretch their legs
But all had time to think.

They brought in cups of Horlicks
And took them to their seats
But when they finished drinking
The Lords were fast asleep.

THINGS TO COME

When a marriage falls to pieces
Give her all that you have got
The house, the car, your treasures
Things that you forgot.

In time you may replace them
A wife you can't neglect
The passing years will tell you
You each will gain respect.

Your children may have children
The house still there to greet
Grandma waits beside the door
To sounds of tiny feet.

When a marriage falls to pieces
and you have to leave, to roam
Remember, its years later
That your children can come home.

GUANTANAMO SOLUTION

Oh, Mr President
I hope you do what's right
The world has changed from bad to worse
Top bankers are in flight
So many banks are closing
Their buildings up for rent
Bring detainees in from Cuba
To solve an argument
A bank could be a fortress
So make them into jails
A place that's fit for terrorists
Completely off their rails
We know it is a problem
But hardly is your fault
Pick out the very naughty ones
Then put them in the vaults.

FROM L.A.

There was a lady from La Mancha.
But this one's from L.A.

Although she speaks some Spanish
　　She comes from far away.
　　She knows a little Russian.
　　He's hairy and quite small.
　　Another guy from England.
　　Much older but quite tall.
　　To her all men are easy
　　She speaks in every tongue.
Prefers them when they're crazy
　　And never quite so young.

THE LEMMING GUIDE

A lemming with a gammy leg
Was way behind the tribe
Who massed upon the clifftop
In an act of suicide

Now grateful for that sudden limp
This wounded lemming is no wimp
Who plans to be a lemming guide
And try to stop more suicide.

ONE TRUE BELIEF

——— •●• ———

There is only one true belief, its, "I am not sure"
God said that to me when he was feeling depressed.
He said, "It's alright for you.
I have to live light years from anywhere and I am
surrounded by the dead."
I said to him, "Oh I do believe in you"
He said, "Ah, You are only saying that
to cheer me up."

EVERY DAY

Every day is much the same
He lives alone and feels a pain.

Every day the Carer comes
To wash the parts as did his Mum.

Every day he cries to sleep
Then hides his shame beneath the sheets.

A WORM

A worm lives in my flowerpot
In his little orange home
No worm friends, or neighbours
Just lives there all alone.

He really longs for company
A woman worm, a Betty.

I've done my best to help him
With a can of Heinz Spaghetti.

GOODBYE & RUN

It's so easy to say goodbye
Pick up the phone to tell the guy
Just practice words sometime before
Then say you can't talk anymore
In 20 seconds the job is done
You're free to go, now free to run

THE DOCTOR & THE WHORE

—— •●• ——

He owned the Doctor's practice
It was next door to a whore.

She didn't need to practice
She'd done it all before.

Men came to see the doctor
But first they called next door.
The doctor knew why they had come
They'd come next door before.

IN THE QUEUE

Like a spider she shivers
Then waits for her prey
Young men are attracted
A price they must pay
She knows what she's doing
And knows what she's got
The clap and the itches
Much worse, she hopes not

Her drugs are a problem
And habits ain't cheap
Drunks can bring business
But give her the creeps
Her clients are local
The town has its cynics
They all wait their turn
In the queue at the clinic.

MAX FACTOR

*Max Factor has a special cream
It makes you look so young
You can shove it almost anywhere
Except your eyes and bum.*

*Max Factor's Anti-Ageing Cream
Can smooth the years away.*

*I tried it on the parrot
It died of shock that day.*

*Max Factor's Anti-Ageing Cream
I buy it by the trolley.*

*It keeps me looking very young
I miss my bird called Polly.*

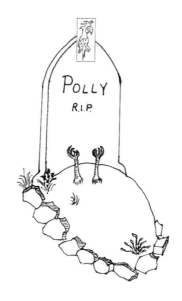

TWICE

If you could live your life again

And everyone did too

There'd be twice as many people

And twice as many you.

BELIEVE IT OR NOT

Believe in what you want to believe,
but its best not to want to believe.
Then what you believe will be what you
believe and not what you want to believe.
To believe what you want is what you want
and not what you want to believe.
If you believe this you'll believe just about
anything you want to believe.

MAKE AN ANT

—— ·•· ——

Imagine, if you were a God.
Start right now, so make an ant.
Let it worship you and sing.
Make it preach a holy rant.

Watch it kneel to you in prayer
Never quite knowing if you are there.
Could a God do this to you?
Or do you have a different view?

THE CITY RATS

The city rats are smart 'round here,
They read from trash and litter.

Young rats when schooled begin to learn,
Then speak in City Titter.

Their Shakespeare's are McDonalds,
Kentucky Chicken too.
The scrolling words from beer cans,
Encase a pungent brew.

We pay their education,
By throwing junk and tins,
The rats are taking over,
So throw your trash in bins.

LE CRAP HOTEL – PARIS

We remember it well at the Le Crap Hotel
Rebuilt for the French Foreign Legion.
Thin blankets and sheets – not changed for some weeks
Had designs from a wine growing region.

We'll remember it well at the Le Crap Hotel.
Its bathroom was cold like a freezer.
Shower taps were all smashed so we gave them a bash
Then water shot out like a geyser.

We left the hotel, to the sound of noon bells.
Down payment was lost. They were winners.
A beggar came by with a glint in his eye.
Then gave up his pie for our dinner.

This Paris hotel, has no stars you can tell
Except stars, that are high in the sky.
Beware if you pick it, you're tough if you stick it.
To stay there for long you may die.

MIND GAMES

There are no spells: We know too well.
Nor hells to blame or taunt.

The mind plays tricks and so transfixes
Your flairs you need to flaunt.

Glean from the mind what's so sublime.
Some thoughts, some old, some new.

Whatever is inside your head
These thoughts are only you.

DON'T BE ASHAMED TO CRY

The light can see your tears.
Don't be ashamed to cry.

Only an angry heart
Can drain those tearducts dry.

Don't be ashamed to cry.
Through dampened eyes and mist.
When light recedes and fades away.
Perhaps then you'll be kissed.

EPILOGUE

One day when I am gone,
they'll read this poem.
It's not too long.
Instead of wondering what to say,
or where to look,
they'll find my book.
More words, I must convey.
Not hard to say,
this is my day.
I thank the world,
For what it's done for me.
My children and my family.
So now I've gone.
The baton passed, now carry on.
Then do what's right, be strong.
In life I tried,
So carry on with pride.

In 2002, a colleague at work had a new girlfriend and it was Valentine's day. He had a large card which he wanted to take to her during his lunch break but he could not find suitable words to write. To help out I wrote down a few words on a piece of paper which he then copied onto his card. After a much longer than normal lunch break, he came back to work with a large grin on his face. Apparently she was impressed, she said, "I never knew you could write words like this, did you do it yourself?" "Of course," he said. She took him to bed. Until that moment I don't think I had ever tried to write in verse or rhyme, it worked for them.

LOOSE SCREWS

Eric C. A. Godward was born in Runcton Holme, Norfolk, England, in Nov. 1940. In 1946 the family moved 70 miles to the coastal town of Felixstowe, in Suffolk where he spent his school years.

On leaving school he became an Apprentice Metal Pattern Maker, then carried on in engineering to become a Technician in the Royal Air Force on a nine year engagement. During his service time he had one year tours to both Australia and Canada. After leaving the R.A.F. he joined a company which manufactured machine tools for the semi-conductor Industry.

Eric has now had over 50 years of engineering experience and this has included 14 years working for himself designing and building his own machine tools. For the past 10 years he has lived and worked in Coventry in the West Midlands.

Occasionally he still gets called out to fix and repair machines but this is much less frequent these days so there is time to write the odd verse and rhyme.